T0354429

LYAH! LYAH! PANTS ON FYAH!

The Stories, the Lies, and Steps to Sacred Healing for Adult Survivors of Childhood Sexual Abuse

Lou Bishop

Balboa Press books may be ordered through booksellers or by contacting:

Balboa Press
A Division of Hay House
1663 Liberty Drive
Bloomington, IN 47403
www.balboapress.com
1 (877) 407-4847

Print information available on the last page.

ISBN: 978-1-5043-4108-0 (sc)
ISBN: 978-1-5043-4110-3 (hc)
ISBN: 978-1-5043-4109-7 (e)

Library of Congress Control Number: 2015915913

Balboa Press rev. date: 11/10/2015

"Our families provide the foundation for our identities by modeling a blueprint which can impact our destiny for better or for worst. A dysfunctional family cannot help but impart a dysfunctional foundation. The offspring in such a family are not afforded the healthy, proverbial wings necessary to soar. The good news is that with knowledge, the right tools and the courage to follow though we can become empowered to change our destiny."

John Bradshaw, The Family: A New Way of Creating Solid Self-Esteem

TABLE OF CONTENTS

Who This Book Is For x
Preface xii
Who I Am 1
Hurting People Hurt People 3
The Reality of Statistics 6
What Is Child Sexual Abuse? 8
Types of Abuse 9
Your Life Is Whispering to You 11
People Pleasing; Lack of Boundaries and the Rescuer Syndrome 11
Unhealthy Choices in Partners 12
Low-grade Depression 12
Relationship Remix 13
How Desperate Are You? 15
The Diaries 18
    The Counting Game 19
    Kidnapped and Brainwashed 21
    Just Three Words 23
    Left for Dead 26
    Trapped 28
    The Call Girl 29

The Family that Prays Preys on their Own 32
Mother Dearest 33
What If? 36
I Thought You Loved Me 37
I Am A Mother 39
The Black Hat 42
Spiritual Healing 45
This is my Story, this is not my Life! 47
Steps to Sacred Healing 51
Before We Begin 52
Self-Esteem 52
Codependency 53
Toxic Shame 54
Leave Your B.S. at the Door 56
You are Not Your Story 56
So What's Your Story? 56
Surrender 58
The Power of Love and a Supportive Network 58
Prayer and Meditation 59
Ten Lies that Imprison You 60
Lie I I Am Not Good Enough 61
Lie II I Am Powerless – Nothing Will Change 62
Lie III It was My Fault; I Am Bad 63
Lie IV I Have to Earn Love and Acceptance 64
Lie V I Have to be Perfect 65
Lie VI Being by Myself Means that I Will be Lonely 65
Lie VII I Need Someone Else to Complete Me 66
Lie VIII When I Get ______________,
I'll Be Happy 67

Lie IX I Need to be Nice Rather than Authentic 67
Lie X I Am Cursed and Damaged 68
The Key to Sacred Healing is Forgiveness 69
Forgive Them – They Had No Idea 70
A Few Things About Forgiveness 70
The problem 72
The solution lies within the problem. The solution is forgiveness. 72
Acknowledge Your 'Isness.' 74
What Is Acknowledgment 74
Seek Spiritual Counseling 75
Create a Family Tree (Genogram) 76
Avoid premature confrontation. 77
Identify your feelings non-judgmentally. 77
Avoid making excuses for the perpetrator. 79
Trust the recovery process. 79
Affirm the new you. 80
Make a Daily Investment in Your Growth. 81
Forgive yourself. 82
Cultivate Perpetual Gratitude. 82
Create a Power Playlist. 82
Reward Yourself. Celebrate Life. 83
Diet and Exercise. 83
Set Boundaries. 84
Renewal and the Transformed Mind. 85
My Forgiveness Letter 86
Conclusion 89
Five Things Never to Tell a Sexual Abuse Survivor 91
Everything happens for a reason. 91

That happened a long time ago. 91
I understand how you feel but … 92
Everything is going to be all right. 92
Just Stop Thinking About It. 93
30 Empowering Affirmations 94

WHO THIS BOOK IS FOR

This book is for you. This book is for your daughter. This book is for your sister. This book is for your niece. This book is for your girlfriend. This book is for your wife. This book is for your mother and your grandmother. This book is for the survivor of childhood sexual abuse and/or anyone who loves them.

***

If you have survived childhood sexual abuse, the following symptoms may ring true for you:

You may have a parent who has been diagnosed as depressed or bipolar;

You blame your parents for your failures;

You over-try yet still encounter repeated and consistent failure or simply stop trying altogether;

You live life on the sidelines;

You are unable to connect emotionally;

You are paralyzed with fear of a God whom you pray to desperately yet cannot summon the courage to follow through with any action;

You are all about 'faith' but no 'works';

You would rather run into oncoming traffic than fall in love yet (secretly) desire love and true intimacy; or

You find that everything seems to be falling apart in your life particularly when it comes to relationships, due to memories of incest.

PREFACE

Statistics show that one in three women have been impacted by incest. Despite appearing to be successful, my soul was broken and my heart was bleeding. I'd even made a decision to end my life if the pain did not stop. I did not believe that I would live to be 30 years old. I was not having it -- not with this kind of pain. Every day was a struggle just to perform the simplest tasks. My goal is not to placate you with sweet soothing words. Neither is it to seduce you with promises of a magical solution for your pain. The fact that you purchased this book demonstrates a willingness (or a least some curiosity) for self-examination. And possibly you will find the courage to pursue further healing. At least that is my hope. Consider this your starter book towards healing from childhood sexual abuse and/or incest.

*****

> Courage is the most important of all the virtues, because without courage you can't practice any other virtue consistently. You can practice any virtue erratically, but nothing consistently without courage.
>
> Maya Angelou

Chapter I

Who I Am

Make no mistake about it: incest is soul murder. Not only is the child's body violated, but boundaries and trust are demolished. As a result of my own experience with this violation, I had to develop a special way of coping that I now recognize as a form of detachment, numbness, and victimization. This became my "normal."

I am not a therapist. However, as a child, I suffered at the hands of my perpetrator for over four years, and the effects of that sexual abuse would affect me and my loved ones for the next twenty years. I thought that my life was normal, but my pain and depression became so unbearable that I had to examine why I was suffering from such deep psychic pain. I had to examine why, despite my seeming success, there was so much soul torment in my life that resulted in poor choices, heartache, and pain. When I traced the roots of my pain, I discovered that I had all kinds of rage and resentment toward my perpetrator. And I knew that I had to address my psychic wounds if I expected to live the life that God intended for me. I was desperate to thrive—not just survive.

Ironically—and this is key—I was raised in church. Forced to wear a mask, I had to protect myself and the reputation of the family name. The effects of living with dysfunction and the burden of keeping secrets was crazy-making to say the least. The mosaic of Christianity, dysfunction, and incest did nothing to build my self-esteem or faith in God. The pain of being counted among the "beloved," yet being raped repeatedly by one of the beloved, was ironic. As a young girl, I had no idea how to navigate those dark, emotional waters. I wasn't even sure I wanted to be in the same heaven with the so-called "beloved."

My biggest concern with church was not only the hypocritical nature of the lives lived by the beloved but the inability to share one's truth in a safe place. There was always talk about not fornicating and keeping one's temple holy. And there was talk about forgiveness, yet human sexuality was never discussed—much less incest and childhood sexual abuse—*ever!*

There were so many questions that needed to be answered. Where was God when I was being raped nightly by one of the beloved? Where was I to go if God could not protect me? The most horrific question was how could God forgive such a thing? And if He did forgive and I chose not to forgive, then who would actually stroll through those pearly gates?

These were the crippling questions that my eleven-year-old self had to grapple with, which would cause me to experience immobilizing shame and guilt for years and years.

HURTING PEOPLE HURT PEOPLE

My journey to recovery started by acknowledging what happened and then recognizing the issues and the ripple effects of those issues. The hard work really began when I started to claim, sort out, grieve, and discard my own emotional baggage. I learned that hurting people hurt other people, albeit unintentionally. This was the key to redirecting my anger toward my perpetrator. No. It did not excuse or condone his actions. However, it created a space within which I could better focus on my own healing. Instead of focusing on retribution and hate, I was able to focus on recovery and healing so much so that I facilitated healing workshops for other survivors. I confess that I was surprised and saddened to discover that so many other women like myself from all walks of life were sexual-abuse survivors.

I discovered through my many workshops that numerous women have experienced incest and childhood sexual abuse yet despite being "saved," were living lives of quiet desperation. They were completely paralyzed and unable to live truly authentic lives. Like me, their efforts to live fulfilled lives were thwarted by dark memories, toxic shame, and the inability to share their stories in a safe place. How could they live authentic lives when the very (patriarchal) churches they attended did not provide a safe place or counseling for these and other taboo issues like domestic violence and rape.

Some of these women have agreed to share their precious stories in this book. Some of the stories are longer than others. I urge you not to compare the horror in each story. Just recognize that pain is

immeasurable, and in the case of incest and sexual abuse, God alone truly bottles up the tears of those who have been affected. Be aware that sexual abuse affects every family member, as the family unit is forced to adjust to the horror. The sisters or brothers who witness the act often suffer unimaginable psychic pain.

My primary goal for writing this book is to raise awareness about the devastating reality of childhood sexual abuse and its influence on adult survivors as well as to provide a roadmap for healing. I hope that as these pages unfold, you will gain a better understanding of the aftermath of incest and childhood sexual abuse and also learn how to address some of the lies that survivors are prone to believe.

This book is written for the wounded inner child of every adult incest survivor who desperately needs to be heard, understood, and comforted. And as you read, note the desperation in each word as these precious souls (including myself) seem to cry out for the only things that matter: acceptance, redemption, and soulful love.

I don't care how old you are, the wounded inner child can manifest in negative ways unless your wounded self is acknowledged. Your wounded inner child needs someone somewhere to say:

I hear you!

I see you!

That was a bad thing that happened!

But that bad thing *does not make you bad*.

You suffered a violation and you can recover!

You are not alone!

Chapter II

THE REALITY OF STATISTICS

As I mentioned before, studies show that, in the United States alone, as many as one out of every three girls is sexually abused. That means that you (or someone you know) has been victimized. I hope to provide useful information about how to identify conflicting and painful feelings for adult survivors who have not examined the "soul murder" of abuse. I hope to help adult survivors understand that these childhood secrets may affect all intimate relationships, including sexual and familial relationships, without their realizing it.

I hope to empower you (or someone you love) to come out of the emotional shadows and get your voice back. I also hope to empower you to improve your relationship with God, yourself, and others.

Just to be very clear, in sharing the stories of these precious souls, including my own, my personal goal is not to vilify my perpetrator. In my case, I am clear that my perpetrator was my greatest teacher in the grand scheme of life. I am certain that hurting people actually hurt people. God has caused me to thrive in the "area of my affliction." I am thankful only because I have arrived at a place

in my life where I can say I am healed. I am thankful for the wisdom of the Holy Spirit to implement the most powerful healing tool in the world—forgiveness. I am now empowered to interrupt the sins of the fathers, so to speak. Everyone is tasked with doing his or her own spiritual work, and I believe that this book is part of the work that I am to complete. I am not what happened to me.

Chapter III

WHAT IS CHILD SEXUAL ABUSE?

Child sexual abuse is a violation of power perpetrated by a person with more power over someone who is more vulnerable. This violation takes a sexual form, but it involves more than sex. It involves a breach of trust, a breaking of boundaries, and a profound violation of the survivor's sense of self. It is a devastating and selfish crime.

The most important thing in defining child sexual abuse is the experience of the child. It takes very little for a child's world to be devastated. A single experience can have a profound impact on a child's life.

Some abuse is of a covert nature and doesn't involve physical touch.

Children are fondled, raped, French kissed, forced to perform fellatio and cunnilingus, forced to watch

sexual acts, and made to have sex with each other. Sometimes abuse is couched in "gentle" cuddling or touches; other times it is violent, coupled with beatings or torture.

Children both hate and love their abusers.

If you haven't been abused yourself, particularly if you grew up in a good home, it may be difficult for you to believe that people molest, torture and sexually abuse children.

Laura Davis, Allies in Healing

***

TYPES OF ABUSE

Types of abuse include: hands-on touching in a sexual way; sexualized hugging or kissing; any kind of sexual touching or fondling; oral and anal sex; masturbation of the victim or forcing the victim to masturbate the offender; sexual intercourse.

Overt Sexual Abuse

This involves voyeurism and exhibition outside or inside the home. An example of overt sexual abuse is a parent who parades through the house in his/

her underwear or is inappropriately clothed in the home in the presence of children, causing them to feel uncomfortable.

Covert Sexual Abuse can be verbal - inappropriate discussions around sex or caretakers demanding to know every detail of a child's private sexual life. Not providing enough sexual information is another form of sexual abuse.

Boundary violations and emotional sexual abuse involve inappropriate bonding of a parent with a child, in other words, treating a daughter like a girlfriend.

Sexual abuse may occur between siblings.

The rule for sexual abuse amongst siblings is "acting out" at the hands of a child three or four years older, and being introduced to sexual behaviors that are age inappropriate.

John Bradshaw, Healing the Shame That Binds You.

***

Chapter IV

YOUR LIFE IS WHISPERING TO YOU

Oprah has coined the term "the Whisper." You may have survived childhood sexual abuse but are you ignoring the whispers in your life that are informing you that some inner work needs to be done? What does your life map look like? Here are some markers that may indicate a need for further examination.

PEOPLE PLEASING; LACK OF BOUNDARIES AND THE RESCUER SYNDROME

If you find it difficult, even impossible, to say no to people, you may be a people pleaser. Even though we are advised to love our neighbors as ourselves, be aware of two important words - 'as yourself.' How can you love others if you don't even love yourself? The inability to say no suggests that you may be challenged in your ability to set boundaries. Are you the first one to step in to 'save' others? Are you subjected to the need for approval from others? Do you alter your behavior to please others? On the other hand, are you a control

freak who ignores the boundaries set by others? These are the soul whispers attempting to inform you that you need help. Are you listening?

UNHEALTHY CHOICES IN PARTNERS

Do you hook up with individuals who are physically violent or emotionally unstable? Or do you prefer the controlling type? Does your significant other treat you with respect and honor? Sexual Abuse Survivors suffer from a heart/head disconnect. We can fall in love easily without understanding why. Low self-esteem can dupe us into choosing partners who treat us with disdain. We choose partners who treat us the way we believe we deserve to be treated. Worse yet, we make excuses for their poor behavior especially if we discover that they had a dysfunctional childhood. We become pitiful emotional "super-heros" who can't even save ourselves or we sit on the sidelines of life waiting to be saved.

LOW-GRADE DEPRESSION

Sexual Abuse Survivors may suffer from low grade to severe depression because incest/childhood sexual abuse is the equivalent of soul murder. How does one recuperate from soul murder? A sense of hopelessness can be so overwhelming that suicide seems like a sweet release. Still many choose slow death. We act out inappropriately. We overeat. We abuse our bodies. We choose destructive partnerships. We become promiscuous. We self-medicate with television, alcohol, shopping, food, overwork, overachieving or drugs. We wound

ourselves daily by failing to care for our spirit (wo)man. We do anything we can to avoid feeling the pain of the abuse we suffered. Ironically, unless and until we feel we cannot heal.

RELATIONSHIP REMIX

> "And when I punish people for their sins, the punishment continues upon the children, grandchildren, and great-grandchildren of those who hate me." Exodus 20:5

The relationship remix for a Sexual Abuse Survivor can be like a bad computer virus that replicates itself. Many of us are hopelessly attracted to members of the opposite sex whose personality traits mimic that of our perpetrators. This is the subconscious at work. No wonder we feel cursed.

This vicious cycle is due to the love/hate relationship we had with the perpetrator, particularly if the perpetrator was our father. Our relationship with daddy models our first love relationship with a man, and good ole dad models extremely negative behavior for future lovers when he abuses us sexually. In addition, because the need for a healthy bond was woefully corrupted, we unconsciously seek for that need to be met in our partners. We look for our fathers in our lovers. For that reason, we unconsciously choose lovers who mistreat and abuse us based on the model that father demonstrated. These significant others fit the model of daddy and may even proceed to sexually abuse our children.

We are constantly on the lookout for Prince Charming to rescue us, never realizing that Prince Charming is in fact Prince Damning, who harbors his own dark secrets. This is how the pathology repeats itself.

***

Chapter VI

HOW DESPERATE ARE YOU?

You may be familiar with the story of a woman in a patriarchal society who suffered physically and certainly emotionally from the effects of what is described as "an issue of blood." According to Judaic Law, a women were considered untouchable during their monthly cycle. So for this woman to experience continual bleeding implied that she was deemed untouchable, anemic, sick, lonely and irrelevant all the time. She had been ostracized due to her issue of blood; an issue beyond her control. Had she been stabbed repeatedly, she would have been rushed to the nearest doctor due to profuse bleeding but her slow, secret hemorrhaging condemned her to a life of abandonment, shame and loneliness. Much like this woman, child abuse survivors have a secret, spiritual issue - a secret wound that unless addressed - quietly bleeds.

Figuratively, I was that woman. None of my relationships were working no matter how hard I tried. Was I cursed? Was I crazy? Perhaps a little of both. I had been forced to live a lie. Forced to wear a mask and completely unable to be authentic. I did not know who I was as my identity was rooted in the toxic shame of incest. And my

religion left no room for 'bleeders' like me. I expended invaluable emotional currency and time sulking in the shadows. I knew that my highly religious church would not tolerate the shaming my abuser who was an upstanding man of God. To expose him meant being possibly stoned to death by the 'righteous' crowd.

Ironically, I thought that my childhood was normal. It was only when I shared my experience with my best friend that I discovered how dysfunctional my life had been. It was only then that I learned that I should be angry about it. It was only then that it registered for me that I had been horribly violated by the one person who was supposed to love, care for and protect me. But worse yet, as an adult, I was unaware of how to identify my pathology and dysfunctional behavior. I was incapable of sustaining appropriate boundaries. Someone had to intervene in order for me to realize that I was reliving my childhood in that respect.

I was allowing others to violate my mind, body and time. You see, I was too busy crying out for love - any kind of love. Due to my woundedness, those who responded to what I can only describe as my howl for love were themselves wounded or exploitative. Like that woman in the Bible, I became desperate and summoned all my courage and determination in order to receive healing. I was tired of towing around the heavy baggage of shame and blame for a horrible act that I had no control over. I was so tired of negative thinking, negative outcomes and a downward emotional spiral. Survival was no longer an option for me. I was determined to THRIVE. More importantly, I vowed that I would not stay silent about the impact of sexual abuse. This notion (call it purpose, if you will) was one that I clung to for dear life. Healing began when I became aware of my

emotionally indigent state. I had to stop blaming and start crawling/walking/sprinting towards restoration, so I took responsibility for my own life and chose to tell my story in order to empower others.

As you read the diary entries from some of the women in my workshops and me, suspend your judgment as we celebrate overcoming histories rooted in shame.

THE DIARIES

THE COUNTING GAME

Me.

(Eleven years old)

"1, 2, 3, 4, 5 …

I can't breathe because he is crushing me. Normally I count but today is not a 'counting day.' Normally I can predict when he is going to do this.

51, 52, 53 …

Normally, the house is empty. Normally there is a certain look or intense silence during dinner or breakfast. Funny that I can use the word 'normal' under such circumstances. This is my childhood 'normal.'

He's still here on top of me, saying that he loves me. Soon he'll be done. It doesn't last very long but it lasts forever in my mind. His body is so big. How does this fit with my little body?

100, 100, 100,

A shudder. A gasp. Extra energy is exerted and now it's over.

"I love you. You know that I love you, right?"

He always says that when it's over.

Internally I scream because those words always make me want to throw up.

“I am gonna kill him next time or myself.”

“We have to hurry up and get dressed to go to church,” he says.

And we will pray before that.

I wonder if anyone knows. I wonder if this is what every young girl has to go through.

“I am gonna kill him. Am gonna kill myself.”

Okay he’s gone.

Once the pain in my chest and back and body stop, I can get up and shower.

He’s gone but he will be back.

He always comes back.

I am eleven.

He calls me Pumpkin.

I call him the crusher.

I call him daddy.

KIDNAPPED AND BRAINWASHED

Anna, New York

(Fourteen years old)

John asked if I wanted to use the bathroom. I nodded, NO!!

John came back; dragged my chair out of the little room that I was in into a bigger room with a round table which had about five chairs to go with it. He kisses me on the forehead. He smells real clean and is wearing a white linen suit.

I am very sleepy. So sleepy. Suddenly I hear what sounds like fifty male voices. They are approaching the room. They are approaching the room THAT I AM IN.

My first thought is 'my hair must be a mess' plus "I am very sleepy." Then I think, 'what are you doing?!!!! You need to get out of here.' It's then that I realize that John has drugged me. I had been in and out of consciousness for the whole time that I had been there.

{Just a few hours prior, I had been walking to the corner store on a hot summer's day. This John dude simply walked up to me, punched me in the head and dragged me to his basement. All I remember is the bright light from the blow.}

"SO WHAT are we gonna do with this little lady, bro?!" A male voice was shouting at John excitedly. I sprung to life to discover four old men (at least old enough to have gray in their beards and heads)

sitting at a table playing poker and drinking. John was sitting with them on the fifth chair. A brown bag with god knows what was sitting on the table next to him.

His response to the question was, "You touch her and I'll F@&@ you up right here and right now!!!" As he reached for the bag, I broke out into a sweat for fear of what was in the bag. He pulled out a big gun and pointed it at the man who had inquired about me. Nothing more was said. Guess that meant the subject was closed. He then turned to me, smiled and said, "I love you."

It is at that moment that I fell in love with John. Just like he said I would.

My own guardian had set the stage for this level of crazy. He had abandoned me. I am clear now that I, like most survivors of incest, had lost my heart/head connection. I was completely incapable of identifying dysfunctional behavior in others or myself. Any demonstration of love, even in the midst of being abused, was enough for me. I was willing to settle for crumbs since I had no idea that there was any other option.

Yes. The stage was being set for me to choose dysfunctional, controlling, possessive, overbearing friends and lovers.

I read somewhere that incest survivors seek to replay past events in hopes of a magical outcome. They hope and expect that they will be rescued one day and actually seek a Prince Charming to rescue them from themselves. No one came to rescue me. Just John.

JUST THREE WORDS

Lynette, New Jersey

'I Luv You'

No three words impact an abuse survivor like I love you.

We were never loved or we were loved inappropriately; boundaries were trampled; self-esteem annihilated. Left to fend for ourselves, we either shut down or exuded the stench of utter and complete neediness.

We grew up foraging for love like hungry wolves. Searching eyes and misinterpreting body language, we were susceptible to:

'dirty' luv;

'crazy' luv;

'nasty' luv;

'one-night-only' luv;

'pimp' luv;

'abuse me' luv; or

'secret' luv.

Players knew that 'just three words' worked like abracadabra as we commenced our genie-like transformation. Like a people pleasing genie, we would commit emotional suicide trying to grant their wishes.

Just Three words. Any wish. Anything you want. As many wishes as you desire just for luv - any luv.

We became pleasers and enablers.

We didn't know. Not consciously. But it was the one thing we had to have in any form until real love came around.

Gimme me luv. Feed me.

Our internal landscape resembled that of a desert. We were like the walking dead. Consuming human flesh yet never satisfied.

The constant yearning was quiet, constant, incessant, persistent and unrelenting.

The HUNGRY INNER child was screaming inside all that time. Screaming for appropriate nurturing. Demanding that we make him/her feel safe.

Yet we ignored that inner child because of that thing "happened so long ago," they said. "Get over it." they said.

Yet the black, cavernous hole in our hearts expanded exponentially through the years, leaving an emotional shell.

For these reasons, adult survivors of sexual abuse are more susceptible to domestic violence because we pick inappropriate partners. Any luv is better than no luv, even if it's crazy.

I LUV YOU.

Just Three Words.

… and so it begins.

LEFT FOR DEAD

Anonymous

If you have been sexually abused, I am here to tell you that you have suffered the ultimate betrayal. It can feel as though you have been left for dead by the side of the road after a car wreck. It's as though no cares. Further to that, those who are aware of the accident act as though it never happened and expect you to do the same, even though you are horribly mangled and disfigured. People expect you to smile, dance and sing. "Things are not that bad," they say. "That happened a long time ago," they comment. And of course, you become self-conscious and even try to work on the 'stiff upper lip' thing. But the emotional hemorrhaging and psychic pain become overwhelming after a while. Furthermore, you beat yourself up for not being able to move past the wall of pain.

This invisible 'thing' that is keeping you stuck or in emotional lock-down is real and needs to be addressed. You have the right to feel what you feel. I am here to tell you that you have the right to take all the time that you need to heal. But make sure that you are actually working on healing and not stuffing those dark emotions that come up for you. If not addressed, the path of your life may unfold in all manner of isms, schisms and madness. The ripple effects can go on for years and generations if this matter is not addressed.

You need to know I suffered all kinds of crazy for so many years. My emotional state was like a Disneyland of rides, characters, parades, yellow brick roads, rabbit holes and magic mirrors. My only saving grace was a desperate belief, suspicion, hope that God would change

His mind about not loving me. I needed to believe that something good would come out of all of this pain. My soul was groaning. My spirit was screaming for just one healing touch. All I needed was just a hint or clue that God was there and I knew that if I found Him, I could explain that this whole thing was not my fault. How could I have been born into such a nightmare? How could my life be so pain-filled and meaningless?

I was left for dead.

TRAPPED

Sandrene, Accra, Ghana

I was trapped. Trapped in an extremely religious home where Jesus was Lord and Satan was the enemy. My guardian substituted as one or the other on any given day. He was my Lord, the provider who fed me, paid my school fees, purchased books and shoes, put clothes on my back and took them right back off. My payment for the good things from my Lord was my own soul. For at least four years starting from the age of ten, I 'earned my keep' by allowing myself to be his 'call girl.'

He would end each session with "I love you and this is our secret." As a ten year old, it was impossible to process these actions let alone dissect his declaration of love. Did these heinous acts and declarations of love go together? Was this to be my life? Was he not supposed to do this with mother? Should I run away? Could I run away? And if I did, where would I go? We had no other family in the U.S. Besides, no one would believe that this great man of God could do such a horrible thing.

THE CALL GIRL

Anonymous

My pimp tells me that I need anger management therapy. Whatever! I think that he is the one that needs it. I am fine. I grew up in a religious family but was turned off by the strict routine and incessant declarations that I was a sinner and what not. It did not seem as though anything was actually changing. In fact, my father used to rape me on a daily - make that nightly - basis to the point where I thought every little girl went through that. I actually thought that was normal.

I guess that is why I decided that I would never get married and never have children. Men always hurt you and they always leave you so I knew that I would not set myself up to be hurt, lied to and cheated on all over again. Nope. I knew the deal then and I know the deal now. I am playing the 'love' game to win. Men will be paying me for my time because I have already had my soul ripped apart. I have nothing left to give a man and even if I did - I wouldn't give them nothing.

I've seen it a million times so why would my life be any different. All men are dogs too. And they are completely incapable of loving anyone but themselves.

And yeah. I was what they call 'in love' once. All I got was a bucket full of my own tears; heartache and pain. I gave him everything and he just used me up. So that's why I am using them now. They will never get the chance to use me again. They will pay for my cars,

houses and jewelry and I will invest absolutely nothing but a little time, conversation and sex. That's it. Good-bye and good riddance.

I admit that I do get tired of giving my body away like that but nothing else is going to give me the kind of money that I am used to. And I do feel lonely sometimes.

Sometimes I wonder if anyone could love me - the real me. It gets real lonely sometimes with no one to love and trust or really talk to. I can't admit that I need someone in my life to love me. That idea will weaken me. I need to be strong and detached.

Don't judge me. You don't know anything about me. My father raped me almost every night for at least seven years from the time that I was six years old. I ran away because I just couldn't take it anymore. I just couldn't. I was lucky. I met a nice man who ran an escort service and the rest is history.

Clients ask for me by name all the time. That's how amazing I am and all that I do is give them the compassion and kindness that I never got. That's what men respond to. It's funny that I give away the one thing that I never received. The one thing that I will never get. The one thing that I needed then and now.

But I can't admit that to myself else I'd go insane. Maybe I am already insane. I don't know.

I have no place to belong other than with the other escorts. Most of them are washed up, tired and bitter. I hope that I don't become

like one of them. I desperately need a safe, peaceful place to belong. I am haunted by so many dark memories. I am so tired. So tired.

I wish I'd never been born into that family. Perhaps my life would have been very different.

Sadly I allowed the sins of my father to be visited upon me.

Regardless of the fine clothes, cars and jewelry, my life is a living hell.

I can't take one more guy telling me about his freaky fantasies.

I need a place to rest.

I am so tired.

I am so angry.

I am so lonely.

But I am fine.

THE FAMILY THAT PRAYS PREYS ON THEIR OWN

Helene, Jersey City

One Sabbath (we were Seventh Day Adventists) as we kneeled to pray (after he had raped me earlier that morning) I began to weep uncontrollably. The prayers simply became more fervent while I sobbed uncontrollably until my throat was dry. At that moment, I decided that God either did not exist or simply did not care about me. But how could that be? All the Bible stories about Daniel in the lions' den, or Samson's supernatural strength or Moses parting the Red Sea must mean that some sort of miracle could be worked out for me. Even a mini-miracle would do. But that miracle never happened. I waited and waited but it never came. That's why I am now an atheist. Not much more to say here.

MOTHER DEAREST

Anonymous

It seems as though my mother was angry/depressed all the time. I was convinced that either she did not love me or I had been adopted and she had simply changed her mind about the adoption. Between the sexual abuse from dad, the perceived disdain from my mother and fire and brimstone from church, I thought I would go insane. Maybe I had. Gone insane, I mean.

My mother was perfect in my eyes. She always smelled divine. She was the most beautiful woman in the world to me. I was never able to feel her love. My mummy; this divine, sweet-smelling, ethereal being never condescended into my little space. Don't get me wrong. I need to be clear that I was well provided for as a child. On the surface, everything appeared to be perfect; but emotionally I was suffering from PTSD. (I did not know that there was an actual name for the kind of stress that I was experiencing.)

Mummy was never able to verbally express her love until many, many years later when I was well into my 30's. What I know now is that she had her own story and her own issues to grapple with. Sadly, I still don't know her stories.

My mother was a nurse. She worked most weekends. Me too. Every Saturday that she worked, I worked.

Here is an excerpt from my diary.

> *The front door just closed so I know that Mummy has just left for work. My heart is beating faster and faster because I know what is coming next. Within 15 minutes, I see his shadow beneath my bedroom door. It's time. I can smell him. It's a smell that I will never forget as long as I live. Sometimes it's over quickly. But it hurts every time. It hurts in my body. It hurts in my heart and it hurts in my soul because I know that no one will help me … EVER.*
>
> *When he is finished, I can feel the wetness and want to throw up. But I dare not because if I do, he'll simply become infuriated. I feel the wetness. And it has a smell which I will never forget.*
>
> *"I do this because I love you," he says. "You know that I love you right?"*
>
> *"Now get washed up or we'll be late for church."*
>
> *So I do. I take a shower and don the beautiful clothes and shoes that I have 'earned.'*
>
> *We then gather around in a circle along with my beloved little brother. We hold hands and pray and thank God for the Sabbath.*
>
> *I feel ashamed because the Sabbath brings me pain.*

One night I came home late from school and my father asked me where I'd been. He felt that I had been out with a boy. I replied, truthfully, that I had stayed late to study for an Algebra final. He remarked, "I can actually have you tested to see if you have been with some boy."

I responded angrily, "Go ahead …" then I can tell them about how you were my first man!" He winced. In that moment, I cringed because those words crystalized the horror of my existence. My intention to hurt him with words had backfired.

The very next day we went shopping for shoes. I was being rewarded for my compliance. This was a habit really. Every other week my father would take me shopping for clothes and shoes or anything I wanted. No price was too high.

I can only imagine how angry/hurt this must have made my mother. Perhaps she had already suffered in her own way and had learned to be helpless.

In the meantime, I was being taught how to be a 'good girl' and a 'good woman.' He was teaching me to stuff my feelings and be complacent. She was teaching me about co-dependency and learned helplessness. The religious, patriarchal mold was being set. Men and their needs mattered more than those of little girls.

Later on I would come to understand how incest impacts the whole family, not just the one who is actually being raped.

WHAT IF?

Anonymous

I wonder what my life would have been like had I not been abused. So many wasted years of self-hate and self-doubt have gone by. By the time that I came to myself, I was nearly 40 years old. This is my biggest regret.

I THOUGHT YOU LOVED ME

Beverly, San Diego

I thought that you loved me. I gave you everything. And the more that I gave the less I got. The more that I tried to please you, the more you took me for granted. You exploited me and abused me and left a hole in my heart.

Why don't you love me? Why can't you love me? What do I have to change to make you love me? What do I have to do? Who do I have to be?

Am I not good enough for you? When we first met, you said that you loved me. You said that I was everything that you ever wanted in a woman. You said that I was your soul mate and the love of your life. So when we moved in together, I thought that things would get better; I thought that we would eventually get married and start a family.

I gave you my body and shared dreams with you. I shared all my pain and brokenness with you - all the pain of my uncles and brothers raping me repeatedly over the years. The pain and fear of not feeling safe to tell anyone - just you. I shared the pain of my mother's abuse too. Nobody ever really loved me just for me.

I never felt beautiful. I never felt attractive. I always prayed for someone to rescue me from my family, my pain and my life. But no one ever came - until you. You knew what to say to make me

feel loved, desired and safe. You said that you loved me. And I believed you.

So I worked hard at two jobs to buy your love. After all, love is not free, is it? Love has to be earned, worked for and bought and sold but it is never ever free. At least not for me. All my life I've had to fight for any good thing. I had no time for depression or sadness. I could not live there. I had to stay strong and fight because nobody ever did nothing for me. I always found myself in situations where I received the short end of the stick.

For three years our love was perfect. You filled me up completely. Your love was all that I needed.

And then you changed suddenly and unrecognizably.

When you first hit me, I convinced myself that you were just having a bad day. I prepared a special dinner for you. You bought me flowers and we made the best love ever.

But your physical and verbal abuse escalated to the point where I was constantly walking on eggshells whenever you were home. Everything became a problem for you. I got the sense that you despised me but your apologies suggested that things would get better someday.

The doctor says that I am lucky to be alive. The stitches in my head will heal in time but I still can't believe that you stabbed me there. You should know that I would do anything for you still. I would forgive you anything. Anything. How can I make it better?

I AM A MOTHER

Cindy – Trinidad, West Indies

The doctors have given me Zoloft, Lexapro and Paxil (paroxetine). The attendants are nice to me. I spend most of my days just sitting around. I am afraid of the other patients in this psychiatric ward. Some of them are violent but my roommate protects me. She repeats the phrase "I don't take no sh@@" all day long. Even though she seems to always be angry she is very kind to me and even protects me from the others.

I fear the night most of all because that is when I remember everything that I have done wrong as a mother. Maybe God has caused me to have this nervous breakdown. Perhaps it's my punishment.

When my daughter comes to visit me, I feel ashamed, pitiable and grateful all of at once. I am amazed that she comes to visit me.

You see, I never wanted children and I was depressed throughout my pregnancy. I sent her to live with relatives shortly after she was born and her father insisted that she come to live with us at the age of eleven. I agreed just to please him.

I never bonded with her. I don't think that realized then how I was in fact abandoning her emotionally. I am clear about that now. I always wanted the best for her. She is my daughter after all.

At night I think about how I betrayed her.

When she told me that her father (my husband) was sleeping with her, I did not want to believe it. The first thing that came to mind was hiding this from the world.

Sadly I never considered leaving him and when he said that she was lying, I knew that he was a liar. But he was my husband. What would people think?

I was numb when I took her to the abortion clinic those two times. I punished her by disallowing general anesthesia. I wanted her to feel the pain of aborting their child.

I abandoned you and I too abused you and I have to live with the burden of that knowledge. Oh God forgive me.

One day all the betrayal simply came crashing down on me.

Oh daughter, I am sorry that I chose my husband over you. I did not feel as though I had a choice. Where would I go? Who would I tell? And most of all - what would people think?

At no time did I consider rescuing you, my only daughter.

And now I am thankful for your support.

Even though you visit me on a daily basis, secretly I plead with you "don't leave me daughter" and then I remember the many times I left you.

I don't believe that I deserve your visits, your love or your forgiveness. But I am thankful that you have the courage to be who you are in spite of who I was.

God help me. I never deserved you.

THE BLACK HAT

Me.

When I first heard of my father's death, I shed two tears, not because I did not love him but because I could not recall any good memories at that moment. But I did weep many days after the funeral because I had lost the father that I never understood. I experienced many emotions. I was confused, numb, sad, scared, nauseous, then confused again. Then I started to worry about the fact that I was not feeling enough sorrow.

Finally, I searched frantically for good memories, or any sliver of some little thing to remember him by. What was his legacy?

My mother asked me to buy her a black hat for the funeral and it was New Year's Eve. Where would I find a formal hat on New Year's Eve? All I knew was that even if I had to make a hat with my bare hands, I would find me a hat. I measured the hats that she already owned. I had to have the correct measurements. I dare not fail this test. I was fighting for my self-esteem after all.

You have to understand my mother's love was my last hope. I desperately desired her love, her approval and her blessing. Psychologists would put it like this - I was never able to mirror my mother or something like that. When I was a child, she never smiled when I walked in the room. She never extended her hand to me to touch me lovingly. How I longed for her touch. I love you mommy. I love you so much. Why can't you love me back? I need you to say it.

So be very clear that the black hat represented a golden opportunity to acquire the one thing that meant anything to me - her love. Maybe now I could win her love. Maybe now, with the black hat, she would see me for me.

By some miracle, I found a hat and it was beautiful! Perfect for her. So when I landed on the island, I just knew she would thank me and hold me close, allowing us the opportunity to bond deeply as we mourned the death of my father – her husband.

When I arrived, there was no smile. Perhaps she was overcome with grief. There was no hug back. I persevered knowing that I possessed the key to abundant love. I had my secret weapon. The Black Hat. I was confident that I could extract pure mother love from that heart of hers. After we settled down and when the time was right, one of my aunts inquired, "Did you bring the black hat?" This was the moment that I had been waiting for my whole life.

I proudly produced the magical black hat fully expecting heaven and angels to come down.

"TA DAHHHH!"

There it was, poised in my brown, quivering, expectant hand. The black hat.

Silence (the suspense was killing me by now.)

I was waiting for what seemed like forever.

My mother examined the hat from afar casually, then said, "I already have a hat in fact. I found one in the closet. Besides your hat won't fit anyway."

I was crushed. Yet with that my emancipation had just arrived.

In that moment I realized that our relationship or lack thereof was not my fault. It was out of my control. I may possibly never be validated by her and that had to be ok. I had to take responsibility for loving myself and honoring her. I had to forgive the fantasy of a perfect mother/daughter relationship. In that moment, I understood that unconditional love meant accepting people (even one's mother) just as they are regardless of whether or not their response to you was way different from what you imagined. I realized then that I would honor and love her because of who she was - my mother.

SPIRITUAL HEALING

Sara, Queens, New York

There I was curled up in a fetal position in the corner of my bedroom, troubleshooting the many ways that I could end my life with the least amount of pain. My heart had been shattered into a million pieces already at 14 years of age. I had lost all hope and worst of all there was no one to comfort me. No one to believe in me. I had been abducted two days before by a crazy pimp and my guardians, though 'happy' to have me back, made it clear that it was 'my fault.' No surprise here, since the incest over the years was my fault as well.

By now, my father had denied all accusations of rape to my mother. "She always had an active imagination," he said. What I know now having lived a little is this: she knew. In fact years later she confessed to feeling overcome with guilt because she had done nothing to protect me. She had chosen her man over me. I had been forsaken.

While plotting my own death in my princess pink (I kid you not; this was a real color) bedroom, I heard a little voice which said EAT. Truth is that I had not eaten for days. Yet eating was the last thing on my mind. Still, this gentle voice persisted "EAT. Eat my Word."

Having been raised in an extremely religious family, Bibles were scattered through the house like ticker tape. Laughable isn't it. Bibles everywhere not a saint in sight.

I obeyed the voice by crawling to the night stand. Inside was a notebook, my diary and a King James Bible.

My intention was to write a suicide note.

The most pivotal moment in my life was just about to happen! Because I was so teary-eyed and sweaty, the bible slipped out of my hand as I removed it from the drawer.

This is how the Message Bible puts it …

"Ps 27:10 - My father and mother walked out and left me but God took me in."

BAMM!

(I get choked up when I recall the verse that the Bible opened to.)

Those words touched me to my core. I cried and cried and cried. So many tears. What a release. Actually, what a relief. Perhaps God *did* care about me after all.

You have to understand, I was facing what I thought was the end of my life. In my darkest moment, here was what seemed like a direct message just for me - the Forsaken and Abandoned. I have never been the same since that day. That is the day that healing began.

This is my Story, this is not my Life!

Anonymous

When one tells a story it consists of so many details. The question is whether or not you allow the story to mold your life and your actions or whether you use it for growth and empowerment.

A little girl laughs as she hugs her mom. Full of energy as she gazes into her mother's eyes, she smiles. There is innocence in her eyes as she gently strokes her index finger down her mother's cheeks.

We all can envision that little girl, especially in ourselves. That is one memory I will always have and can always jump back to as a nine year old. This memory makes me feel protected, loved and cherished. The rest of those memories are not as joyful and happy as I wish they could have been.

I look at other children who are nine years of age and I see them full of energy, their laughs as their moms hold them. The look on their faces as they gaze into the eyes of their mothers. I pray there will be more moments like that for them throughout their years. I pray that they never have to experience moments of an older cousin asking them to play house and then having their innocence taken away in such a short time

I can recall being in a 6th grade sex education class. For some reason, the teacher mentioned something in regards to sexual abuse and I broke down at my desk. It was not the first time she had mentioned the topic but it was the first time I allowed myself to hear it. She

escorted me outside and asked if someone had touched me. With all the fear in my heart I said 'Yes'. Little did she know that it had happened just prior to class. It had been happening for almost a year, in fact.

This man knew my mother and he was nice to our family but I was accustomed to being viewed as nothing but merely a "sexual object" for men.

I remember sitting in a judge's chambers while my case was being adjudicated. I felt I was the one who was being convicted. The look on his lawyer's face asking me if I was sure I didn't like him or was I sure I didn't have a crush on him infuriated me.

I knew then I would never be a lawyer nor did I ever want to be. How can you ask such a question after what this man did to me? Why did I have to sit in there and try my best to recount the multiple times he touched me and how he touched me. Isn't that what the police report was for? Why was I on trial for keeping his secret? Why did I have to recount the worst day of that entire experience when he took me in the back in the bathroom by the wooden door whispering how much he loved me and that he couldn't live without me. Why should I recount how he pulled my pants down and opened his zipper and inserted his penis into me. All I could do was shut my eyes and recall the first violation by my cousin. This is my Story, this is not my Life.

He was put in jail for only a year. Blame, shame and guilt became my everyday norm. I was hurt and I wanted to hurt back. Though these two experiences impacted me greatly, I became accustomed to other individuals touching me, whether it was once or twice.

By the time I entered college, I was still carrying the guilt, shame, rejection and un-forgiveness I had with me from that very first incident with my cousin. It was a heavy load. I walked like a confident, sexy and strong lady from the outside, knowing on the inside I was in a bad place. Though I knew I was hurting, I didn't want anyone else to hurt like me. I desperately wanted to help others because I myself was crying out for help. Relationships with guys became scary to me. I didn't trust. By this point I had slowed down in my promiscuity because in college I didn't want a reputation. I encountered a guy that I knew wanted me sexually but I toyed with him. I teased him. I made him wait but when I gave in, he looked in my face a few days later and said, "A man has to do what a man gotta do" and walked away from me. He conquered me. No matter how long it took, he got it! Before I walked, away he walked away. That moment destroyed me. At the age of 22, I stopped my sexual escapades. This is my Story. This not my Life!

Throughout my journey as a victim, the one thing I never allowed myself to do was cry. I never cried about the hurt I was feeling. I never cried about the rejection I felt. I never cried about the love I never felt. I never cried about my pain. I never cried about myself. Crying meant vulnerability to me and I couldn't take the chance to allow myself to be vulnerable, fearing it's what those men saw and that is what gave them permission to hurt me.

My healing came when I laid face down in a circle of women and cried my pain away and finally handed the hurt and pain over to God. I was free not because I handed it over to God but I no longer accepted responsibility for a hurt that wasn't caused by me. I had forgiven everyone but never FORGAVE MYSELF. I carried guilt

that almost destroyed me for secrets that were never mine to keep. I no longer allowed myself to remain a victim but rather at that moment I allowed myself to experience VICTORY! This is my Story. This is not my Life!

Yes, I was raped, molested, used, rejected, even denied BUT I am still here. I cannot change the circumstances of my story but I can and have changed how the circumstances are shaping my life. Do I regret what has happened to me? I may not have had it happen that way nor do I wish this on any human being BUT all I know is the girl that was raped, molested, rejected, used and denied … is ME.

May my story impact another to no longer feel as I felt; to know you are loved by God and wonderfully made in His image. Don't keep the dirty secrets any longer. Set yourself free and forgive yourself for a responsibility you had no control over. No longer hold yourself captive. I know where you are. I have been there too but look at where you can be! The other side of victim is VICTORY!

WE ARE HERE TO HELP EACH OTHER RECOVER TOGETHER.

THIS IS MY STORY. THIS IS NOT MY LIFE!

You can't fix what you can't face.

Anonymous

STEPS TO SACRED HEALING

BEFORE WE BEGIN

You have probably noticed several common themes resonating throughout our stories. These affects include Low Self-esteem, Codependency and Toxic Shame. I'd like to provide some brief descriptions of each. We will then examine ten common lies that Sexual Abuse Survivors (and those suffering from low self-esteem) subscribe to and finally we will examine the sacred healing steps.

SELF-ESTEEM

Once upon a time in a land far, far away …

We all love fairy tales and bedtime stories. As children, we happily embraced the fanciful stories of princesses, knights and glass slippers. Eventually, though, we came to terms with the facts of life. We were exposed to real life witches and goblins. Eventually we made up negative stories about ourselves and developed dark, protective thoughts that caused us to lose our way in the forest called life.

Self-esteem is simply the story or stories that we repeat to ourselves about ourselves and the world in which we live. A story can be an account of events, a rumor, a falsehood or a situation. The aphorism "as a man thinketh, so is he," is a reference to self-esteem. James Allen puts it this way: "As the plant springs from and could not be without the seed, so every aspect of a man springs from the hidden seeds of thought." Whatever you think about yourself is what you will manifest. Thoughts inform actions and behaviors. Self-esteem is manifested in everything that you do or say. Your self-esteem is

evident in the dresses or shoes you wear. Your food choices reflect your self-esteem. You are what you believe about yourself. As a Sexual Abuse Survivor, you may have allowed your perpetrator to cast a dark spell over you placing your life on pause. This dark spell causes you to replay your abuse story so that you remain emotionally scarred for years and years.

CODEPENDENCY

Low self-esteem catalyzes the need to compensate for one's perceived defects. This leads to the development of codependent relationships. Loosely defined, codependency is the process of becoming attached to or dependent on someone or something in an unhealthy way. We can develop a codependent relationship with anything. It can occur with work, food, shopping, church, alcohol or drugs. In other words, codependency says, "By myself, I have no value but I have value if you (or it) make(s) me feel good about myself." My definition of low self-esteem is an innate feeling of not being enough; feeling alone and unloved. As a result, we become shackled to external things like cars, houses, work, husbands, lovers or friends and just plain ole stuff.

As survivors of sexual abuse, we were made to feel worthless. As a result, we stumbled through life in quiet desperation. We didn't believe that we deserved any good thing, so we unknowingly attracted perpetrators as mates. We literally sought out bullies who would further abuse us. The aftermath of incest can be intergenerational. Upon further examination, we often discover that our subconscious mind is playing back that defunct story. This old story can lead to

suicidal tendencies, addictions, fear of abandonment, depression and loneliness if not addressed.

TOXIC SHAME

Despite the victim's pitiable attempts at hiding out, toxic shame screams, "I am a mistake and everything that I do is wrong." Think of toxic shame as the bad kind of cholesterol - LDL cholesterol. If unchecked it will kill.

There are two major types of shame: Healthy and Unhealthy.

Healthy shame informs us that we are human and limited. Healthy shame says that we are not perfect, that we will miss the mark and that we should simply accept this for what it is. Think of shame as a kind of grounding force that rings a warning bell letting us know that we will make mistakes or that we need help. This knowledge empowers us to be authentically human. It should be comforting to know that we don't have to work so hard at being perfect.

Unhealthy shame, on the other hand, forces us to live a false life where we place excessive pressure on ourselves to be super-human. The reason we do this is because we believe that we *are* actually a mistake so we have to hide ourselves from society lest they discover that we are not perfect. Not only is this burdensome, it is crazy because none of the people you are trying to impress are perfect. The effect is the opposite of healthy shame, which is an understanding that though we have made a mistake, we ourselves are NOT A MISTAKE.

Toxic shame can drive one to the edge of madness. In my case, I was insatiable. I wanted more of everything. More money, more stuff and more love. I was starving for attention and searching for love in all the wrong places. I did not realize that victims of toxic shame attracted other victims of toxic shame. It's true what they say about misery. It really does love company. Hurt and wounded people attract others like themselves, and they proceed to hurt each other. Shame breeds more shame just as misery loves company. Instead of paying attention to the actual wound, you may be allowing yourself to live life hidden behind a mask.

***

We wear the mask that grins and lies

It hides our cheeks and shades our eyes

This debt we pay to human guile

With torn and bleeding hearts we smile.

Paul Lawrence Dunbar

LEAVE YOUR B.S. AT THE DOOR

I need you to check your B.S. What is your belief system? Be willing to suspend your former way of thinking to achieve your greatness. You may be familiar with the phrase: "When I was a child, I spoke, thought and reasoned as a child." This is a reference to progressive thinking. In other words, you have to release the poor conditioning that you received as a child. Replace protective, defensive thoughts that no longer serve you with empowering thoughts.

YOU ARE NOT YOUR STORY

Your old story provides a sort of blueprint for how you show up in life. As a child, you had to develop certain defense mechanisms to cope with the horror that was your life. Yet those previous defensive behaviors no longer serve you. Here's a common example of reacting based on your old story. You go on a job interview and are positive that you have landed the job. But a few days later, they call to say that it did not work out. Instead of moving forward and pursuing other interviews, your internal dialog goes something like this: "I knew that I would never get that job. That company was too good for me. I never get anything right. What's the point? I'll always be unemployed, etc."

SO WHAT'S YOUR STORY?

What is your story about your abuse? Do you believe that you were to blame? Have you taken on the shame of the event? Do you believe

that you are bad? In order to address the issue of low self-esteem, you have to reframe the story that you have been telling yourself about the event. Bring your awareness to the fact that you were a child. Your choices were limited or non-existent. Someone who was deeply wounded proceeded to rob you of your childhood. You were a victim then. You are not a victim *now.* Choose Empowerment not Victimhood. To become more empowered you have to choose empowering thoughts. In so doing, your self-esteem will improve. But the question is why should you change, right? Well, you will certainly choose to change if you are in enough pain.

There's a story about a dog (which I am sure that you've heard before) who was sitting on the porch with his master. Every now and then he would let out a painful howl. A passerby finally asked, "What's with the dog?" The owner responded, "He's lying on a nail which is apparently piercing his flesh'" The passerby asks, "so why doesn't he just get up off the nail?" The dog's owner says, "cuz he's not in enough pain yet, I suppose."

Are you in enough pain to want to change your life? The only way to go about making this change is to flip your script because your story line forms your world. The only way to change your life is to change your thought life.

You are not your story. You can change.

SURRENDER

Surrender means that all attempts to unravel the mystery of our abuse cease. Stop asking questions like, "why me?" "How come?" and "What if?" We must accept what is. Some people call it accepting our "isness." In order for healing to begin, you must surrender your mind, body and soul to the Holy Spirit. You were not meant to carry the heavy burden of toxic shame and guilt. Surrendering means to lay your burden down. Surrendering means completely releasing your cares and worries to the Omnipotent One. Unless and until you do so, healing will be virtually impossible. Let it go.

THE POWER OF LOVE AND A SUPPORTIVE NETWORK

Once you have surrendered completely to the Holy Spirit, you need to embrace a supportive group of people who will love you, encourage you and hold you accountable. There is healing in community. Your journey should no longer be one of solitude. Yet it's important to extricate yourself from negative relationships. In order to carve out a new life for yourself, you have to be prepared to make drastic changes. This may be challenging. In fact, I guarantee that it will be challenging, but when you cross that bridge to wholeness and look back on your former live you will wonder why you didn't do it sooner.

PRAYER AND MEDITATION

Not only is prayer the most powerful weapon in your arsenal, prayer is your right and your privilege. Prayer empowers and enlightens. Prayer connects you with the God of this great universe. You don't have to be in a special place or position though I recommend a daily practice where you have a special place and time for meditation.

Quiet times with the Almighty can ground you against all the negatives that life can bring. There is a sweet release that comes from spending time saturating in the Bible and praying that cannot be over-emphasized. One healing word from God can change everything. Investing time in prayer and meditation will allow you to rediscover the authentic you as you remove your misconceptions and fears layer by layer.

One of the Hebrew words for meditate is "hagah," which means to murmur, ponder or speak. Speaking God's word to oneself repeatedly emboldens one's faith. Faith will bring about manifestations from the unseen into the seen. With prayer and meditation, we develop keen insight and wisdom in every aspect of our lives.

TEN LIES THAT IMPRISON YOU

LIE I

I AM NOT GOOD ENOUGH

Childhood sexual abuse tops the list of heinous acts that can annihilate self-esteem. Further to that, life can throw numerous curve balls and present unforeseen challenges. If you have suffered at the hands of a sexual predator, you may be suffering from low self-esteem. Even if you are successful in your career or financially, you may be suffering from depression and low self-esteem.

Yet you are still standing. You are still here. You are still fighting. The fact that you are still reading this book lets me know that you are willing to fight to improve your life and relationships. When you work on you, you actually impact everyone around you. When you improve your life, you improve the lives of everyone around you.

You are good enough! You are a survivor. Instead of blaming yourself, start loving yourself. Create a mission statement. Read the Bible and other empowering books. Make it a habit to read at least one empowering book a month. Check out my affirmations and repeat them on a daily basis. Pen some of your own affirmations. Develop a daily spiritual practice. The habit of praying for guidance and peace cannot be overstated.

LIE II

I AM POWERLESS – NOTHING WILL CHANGE

Understand that things are changing all the time. There was a time when you were unable to walk; you simply crawled. But now you are walking and running without giving it a second thought. What happened in the past happened and nothing can change that. You have no control over what happened then but you are responsible and accountable for what happens now. Stop living in the past. Your life is passing you by. You are missing golden moments like time spent with your family and your children. My intention is not to tell you to 'just be happy.' I know for a fact that those words are empty. If we could all 'just be happy" we simply would. But it's not this easy, is it? Who you are and what you do is based on a series of your thoughts and habits. What do you tell yourself on a daily basis? The way that you process things and the stories that you tell yourself must be changed in order for your life to change.

God has given you a Spirit of Power, love and a sound mind. And you have to start believing and accepting this as your new truth.

Write your affirmations down and place them in your wallet. Repeat your affirmations seven times a day and create your own empowering affirmations. The battle is in your mind. If you win mentally you can conquer anything that life throws at you. A strong, powerful mind leads to a powerful life. You have to be courageous enough to change your thought life. If you do so, you will change the trajectory of your life.

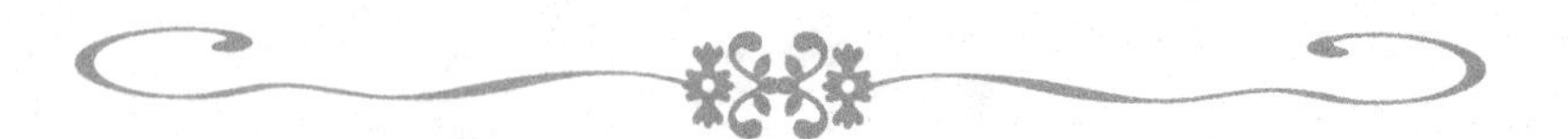

Spend time each day focusing on just one empowering thought. You are loved by an Almighty, Powerful God. You survived the worst thing and now it's up to you to discover your life purpose and fulfill your God-given destiny.

LIE III

IT WAS MY FAULT; I AM BAD

Dear heart! Why would you allow yourself to subscribe to this idea? You were a child and developmentally incapable of understanding what was at stake. You were exploited and taken advantage of when you were most vulnerable. You were incapable of navigating the murky waters of sexual abuse.

As a Sexual Abuse Survivor, I used to blame myself as well. My assailant lured me into his trap by asking me to keep a secret. Maybe yours did too. Before I realized that was happening it was too late. If you are imprisoned by toxic shame, you are creating toxicity in your soul. I am here to tell you that it was not your fault. The act itself was bad. You are not bad. Let me repeat. Something bad happened to you. You are not bad.

LIE IV

I HAVE TO EARN LOVE AND ACCEPTANCE

Sexual Abuse Survivors often feel that they have to work to earn love and acceptance. The soul murder of incest and childhood sexual abuse is such that we grow up feeling isolated, lonely and afraid to be authentic. We were forced to keep secrets and embrace deep, toxic shame. We repeat phrases like "If only he/she/they knew what was going on inside of me (or what happened to me), he/she would be appalled." Even though we love our spouses, children and friends, we may feel detached and fearful. Despite appearing to be social rock stars, we feel terribly lonely, even in the midst of devoted friends and relationships.

As a result of soul murder, we were forced to prove our worth by overcompensating, overworking and overachieving. Those who could not muster the strength to overperform simply committed to underachieving or not trying at all.

Each of us is responsible for loving ourselves then loving our neighbors. If you identify some character flaws that need work, then do the work.

However, you do not have to work to earn love. If you find yourself in relationships that place you in this mind space, get out now. You do not have to prove yourself. You are loved, loving and lovable.

LIE V

I HAVE TO BE PERFECT

Really! The truth is that nobody is perfect. Period. The notion that you have to be perfectly flawless can paralyze and limit your accomplishments and suck the joy and excitement out of your life. Ironically, the pursuit of perfection may cause you to avoid or abandon tasks, goals and dreams, thus creating even more fear. I read somewhere that completing even simple tasks successfully can create a sense of well-being that can propel one to achieve other tasks. I believe that the perfectionism value is rooted in low self-esteem. Instead of trying to be perfect, why not focus on performing or completing your task to the best of your ability.

LIE VI

BEING BY MYSELF MEANS THAT I WILL BE LONELY

Life can be lonely at times. However, loneliness can occur even when you are in a serious relationship or married. So if you are counting on being in a relationship as a magical fix for loneliness you need to revisit that thought. Paradoxically, if you are not content and happy by yourself, you will not attract the right folks in your life. If you don't enjoy being with you, why should anyone else? Besides, some alone time allows you to examine yourself and learn about who you really are. You can take the time to build a career, study, travel and

simply build lasting friendships. In doing so, you will be better able to manage an intimate relationship with healthy boundaries.

LIE VII

I NEED SOMEONE ELSE TO COMPLETE ME

(See Being by Myself Equals Lonely and Empty)

This lie is a close cousin to "Being By Myself Means That I Will Be Lonely." If you fear being alone, you are probably going to attract and hook up with the first big loser that you encounter. You need to work on your self-esteem and it's no surprise because as a survivor of childhood sexual abuse your boundaries were violated in the worst possible way. You may feel needy and isolated, which manifests as co-dependency. Don't worry, though, if you take the time for serious self-examination and proper counseling you can address the root cause(s) and take steps to correct your thought patterns. This particular lie is one of the lies that women in abusive relationships fall for. This lie causes women to rationalize unacceptable behavior from their significant other to their own detriment. Get this. You don't need anyone to complete you. You have been given everything that you need for a successful life already by your Creator.

LIE VIII

WHEN I GET ______________, I'LL BE HAPPY

Girl, you better starting living life now. Waiting for a boyfriend or waiting to lose the last 10 pounds is not the way to go. You need to start loving yourself as you are right now. In so doing, you will attract more love into your life. As they say, happiness is a journey, not a destination.

LIE IX

I NEED TO BE NICE RATHER THAN AUTHENTIC

Being nice does not mean that you are anyone's doormat. Being authentic does not mean that you are not nice. These two characteristics are not mutually exclusive.

You are authentically you! You don't have to please, placate or pontificate to anyone. Being authentically you means that you are aware of healthy boundaries and have no problem with expressing your ideas in a healthy way. Being authentic means that you manifest grace and wisdom in most circumstances because you know who you are.

LIE X

I AM CURSED AND DAMAGED

Dear heart. You are neither cursed nor damaged. You may, however, be suffering from depression, low self-esteem and post-traumatic stress, just to name a few. Earlier in the book, I spoke about the fact that victims of childhood sexual abuse often feel that they are 'bad'. I went on to state that I/you/we are NOT bad. Something bad happened to us and we clothed ourselves in toxic shame.

THE KEY TO SACRED HEALING IS FORGIVENESS

FORGIVE THEM – THEY HAD NO IDEA

A FEW THINGS ABOUT FORGIVENESS

The key to sacred healing is Forgiveness. Forgiveness does not mean that the wrong has been diminished or condoned.

Forgiveness does not erase what happened.

Forgiveness is not a one-shot deal.

Forgiveness does not mean that your perpetrator will acknowledge or even apologize for his/her wrongdoing. In fact, don't waste your precious time waiting for an apology.

Forgiveness takes courage.

Forgiveness is challenging at first and can feel uncomfortable.

Honestly, I was unable to forgive my assailant for a long time. I thought that forgiveness meant condoning his actions. Then I learned that forgiveness was more about my mental and spiritual health. In order to grow past the pain and hurt, I had to forgive or release the past. I had to stop holding a grudge and nursing that old story. It was imperative that I stop replaying those awful deeds in my head.

Forgiveness in no way suggests that you are weak. In fact, it takes incredible courage to embark on this higher path. Without forgiveness,

the focus is downward and negative. Without forgiveness, you remain stuck in the past while life keeps moving forward. Without forgiveness, you will miss out on present opportunities, blessings and relationships.

The problem

The problem is woundedness, guilt and toxic shame. We have to ask ourselves three questions: Is what I am holding onto serving me? Is the anger and the pain enhancing my life? Is this heartache and emptiness empowering me? If the answer to any one of these questions is 'no', then it's time for a change.

The solution lies within the problem. The solution is forgiveness.

I read a story about a man who got a thorn stuck in his foot while walking to another village. After a few minutes of hopping about in anguish, he came to the realization that this was only making things worse. He made the decision to sit down and figure it out and had an 'aha' moment. He realized that he could use another thorn to extract the first. So it is with the mind and so it is with the problem. We suffered severe emotional trauma and as a result we spoke, thought and reasoned in a negative fashion. We believed that we were not worthy of any good thing. We thought we were bad. See toxic shame. Forgiveness releases us to figure it out. It has the power to remove our original thorn.

Forgiveness entails a paradigm shift from what was done to us to our *response* to what was done to us. Sexual Abuse Survivors perform incessant forensics on dead issues in an attempt to understand and/or vilify our perpetrators when we should focus on personal healing and recovery. True healing means implementing the biblical 70x7

forgiveness. In other words, forgiveness needs to become a way of life.

You can't have a positive life with a negative head. And if you have a negative head you will speak and behave negatively. I learned that in order for things to change, I had to change. Someone once told me that until I despised my present, I would never give birth to my future.

Forgiveness means giving up for a change. Forgiveness means acknowledging the truth in order for change to take place.

On the other hand, non-forgiveness means that you are allowing your perpetrator to be your puppet master. You may be familiar with the series "Walking Dead," where zombified (undead) people traverse the earth seeking to devour living victims. This is a perfect analogy of what many Sexual Abuse Survivors experience. We can feel so love-starved, angry or just plain empty that we devour our friends and lovers. And all we are really looking for is a safe place to be. Ironically, even when we find ourselves in 'safe' relationships, our behavior impacts the relationship negatively. For example, some of us are so used to fighting that we create something to fight about since we are not comfortable in a peaceful environment. Don't look now but wherever you go YOU are there.

Your task is to recognize your resistance to non-forgiveness; make the decision to forgive and focus on actually doing it.

ACKNOWLEDGE YOUR 'ISNESS.'

What Is Acknowledgment

> Acknowledgment means being in a state of recognition of what you are thinking or feeling. Acknowledgment is recognition of the truth. Vulnerability, fear, guilt, shame, resentment, or anger, when not acknowledged, will weaken your ability to perceive, respond, and make conscious choices. It is only when you are willing to admit that the feeling exists and that you have a right to experience it that you will be empowered to choose what to do.
>
> Anonymous

The first step towards healing is acknowledging what happened. Yeah – the deeds were heinous. But I am not asking you to try to *understand*. You may never understand but just be willing to acknowledge the facts in the most non-judgmental way possible. Acknowledge the depth of your pain. Know that you are not to blame and that you cannot change what happened in the past. See Serenity Prayer. Acknowledge that you cannot change or control your perpetrator in any way. Acknowledge that you cannot do this alone. Acknowledge that you need the power of the Holy Spirit in order to achieve this high calling.

Seek Spiritual Counseling

Remember that you are a spirit being having a human experience. Deny this truth to your own detriment. Because you are a spirit being, feeding your spirit is a necessary part of sound health. In addition to reading the Bible and other empowering books, you will need someone to assist you on your healing journey. This will spare you unnecessary angst.

Toxic shame will surface and force you into a state of denial at some point. Self-doubt and confusion may set in. You may believe, falsely, that you can do this on your own. Just one question, though, "How has that 'on your own' thing worked out for you so far? If it has not been working out then you need to flip your script right now. Release the idea that you have to be 'crazy' to require a life coach/spiritual counselor or therapist. You need to do whatever it takes to take your life to the next level and this step is crucial.

Finding the right therapist takes time and effort but is worth it. All therapists are not necessarily qualified to deal with childhood sexual abuse and incest.

Here are a few tips:

Get references.

Check out their credentials.

Interview them. (Yes. You have that right.)

Find out if they have actually worked with Sexual Abuse Survivors.

Find out how long have they been practicing and what is their success rate?

Create a Family Tree (Genogram)

The clinical term for a family tree is 'genogram'. Creating a genogram is an important step towards healing, as it will demonstrate patterns of dysfunction in the family. A genogram is a family tree on steroids. It contains information about the physical, mental and emotional state of family members and is often used by therapists as a discovery tool.

It is easy to feel as though your abuse was a random event in the context of the family but more than likely a genogram will assist you in tracing a pattern of some sort of abuse. Studies have shown that sexual abuse and incest are intergenerational. Understanding how you fit in the complex family system will release you from the guilt and shame that you have been carrying for all these years.

If you can interview older family members about that womanizing uncle or grandfather, you may discover more about the family pathology. Listen carefully at family gatherings to off-color jokes. Become a keen observer of behaviors and interactions. Try to recall any known boundary violations, behavior patterns or fondling incidences. Do you remember the room going completely silent

when you arrived just at the moment when family members were discussing another family member? What was that about?

It takes courage, perseverance, even patience to learn about your family's secrets since the goal of the family is to protect the family at the expense of the individuals within the family. Bear in mind that you may never discover the family skeletons, as the secrets are secured in what I call "the family vault." Nothing and noone can wrest the dark secrets from those family members yet alive. And the dead tell no tales. This does not mean that you shouldn't try, however.

Avoid premature confrontation.

Be careful about when, how and where you confront your perpetrator, if at all. Most perpetrators have moved past the incident while you are emotionally stuck in that past event. They may not be prepared to be 'exposed' and may become irate or violent. Be sure that you are emotionally prepared for negative repercussions or a flat-out denial of the event(s).

Be sure that you are emotionally strong enough to deal with the backlash.

Identify your feelings non-judgmentally.

I believe that part of the forgiveness process is releasing all the profound hurt. As Sexual Abuse Survivors we were taught to

keep secrets, stuff our feelings and tell lies in order to protect our perpetrators. Furthermore, we absorbed the shame and blame of the awful acts. We have to re-learn how to express our needs, identify our feelings and give voice to those feelings in a healthy way. Here are some useful tips:

Journal your feelings on a daily or weekly basis for at least two months. If you are not prone to write, record your feelings verbally. Be mindful to keep this sensitive information in a safe place, of course. If you don't feel safe performing the aforementioned tasks, become more aware of your negative self-talk. Do not deny or stuff your feelings. You have probably been denying your true feelings around this and related issues for years. It is important to acknowledge what you truly feel, particularly because your feelings were disregarded during your childhood.

Write a letter to your parents if you feel they failed to protect you.

Write a letter to the parent who abused you.

Write a letter to your perpetrator explaining how you felt about what happened then. And how you feel now. You are not required to mail the letter. This exercise will help you identify your feelings and Re-feel them. You can't heal what you cannot feel.

Write a letter of forgiveness to your Self. See Forgiveness letter.

Avoid making excuses for the perpetrator.

As Sexual Abuse Survivors, we still tend to make excuses for our perpetrators because of the love/hate relationship. Perpetrators often attempt to brainwash their victims with sob stories about never having been loved or trying to convince their victims how much they need them. This manipulative tactic is meant to gain sympathy, thus forcing the victim to keep dirty secrets. Remember that your perpetrator exploited and robbed you of your childhood. Arguably he/she was not aware of the far-reaching impact of the decision to violate boundaries. The collateral psychological and spiritual damage is undeniable and you must recognize your perpetrator's part in the theft of your childhood. That being said, it is imperative that you take responsibility for your life now. You must be courageous and focus on recovery and healing now through examination of the cold facts.

Trust the recovery process.

Your recovery is not unlike the life cycle of a butterfly. Butterflies start off as tiny creatures barely visible to the naked eye. Growth occurs during the larval stage where they multiply in size a thousand fold within a short period of time. Within weeks they evolve from an eggs to chrysalises to caterpillars. As caterpillars, they go through several shedding processes. During the final stages, after eating everything in sight, they search for a place to complete their miraculous transformations wherein they hang upside down. Their change involves the complete disassembly and reassembly of cells

while they are hanging upside down. Now that takes true grit. Throughout your recovery process, you may feel 'up-side-down' every now and again. This is a good thing. When you start to look at the world differently, you are well on your way to transformation. You will soon become a butterfly. Trust your process.

Affirm the new you.

The term "affirmation" is quite popular these days. Affirmations have become a tool for fear management but I challenge you to use affirmations for fear analysis. Use the affirmation process to address the dark whispers in your heart. Speak your truth against the negative whispers that arise for you. Gently analyze the root cause of the fear. Affirm your desire. Declare your intentions and recall your successes in order to maintain integrity with self.

It is imperative that you affirm yourself daily. Words actually inform actions. Proverbs 18:21 expresses the power of the tongue as life-giving or destructive. In the African culture the power of bringing about occurrences by speech is referred to as Afóse (pronounced Ah-fo-shay). You have probably been repeating negative things to yourself for years. Though you can't turn your thoughts off, you can choose your thoughts. Choose empowering thoughts and speak life and healing to yourself. Maya Angelou wrote about words, and her belief is that words stick to the walls, furniture and even clothing and seep into our very being.

For example, if you are angry at an (formerly abusive) aging parent who is now dependent on you for personal care, acknowledge your

anger because what you resist will persist. Examine your anger, then state your intention, which may go something like this: "My intention is to honor my parent in the best way possible despite my past experience with him/her. My desire is to live a life of integrity and forgiveness. And I can do all things through Christ who strengthens and empowers me."

Make a Daily Investment in Your Growth.

Now is the time to invest in your turnaround. Turn off the TV. Get off of Facebook and read an inspirational book like the Bible. Discover and memorize empowering truths that resonate for you. Find autobiographies of people who have overcome adverse circumstances. Read motivational books by Brian Tracy, Jim Rohn or Anthony Robbins, to mention a few. Meditate on the Word first thing in the morning and last thing at night. Create a vision board. Lift yourself up in prayer. Pray for someone else. Make a six month; one year or even a five year plan. Develop the habit of journaling your thoughts daily. Consider leaving a journal for your children to remember you by once you have transitioned. Flood your mind with uplifting thoughts so that you can change your perception and enhance your mental focus. Start enjoying life now. Don't wait for some THING to occur like weight loss or getting that degree or that car or that husband. You are so precious just as you are. Every moment matters.

Forgive yourself.

It's hard to imagine but as Survivors of Sexual Abuse, we blame ourselves for what occurred while we were yet children. We internalize all the shame and guilt that is not actually ours. If you have been blaming yourself, you need to stop the incessant self-judgment, guilt and self-blame. Embrace your journey and lessons therein. James Allen puts it best when he writes that each of us is "a progressive and evolving being." We are where we are to learn and grow. Grow up! Forgive yourself. See Forgiveness Letter.

Cultivate Perpetual Gratitude.

Develop an attitude of gratitude. Write a gratitude list on a daily basis. Everyone has something to be grateful for. Dig deep. You will come up with something. The reason gratitude is so effective is because whatever you focus on expands. Focusing on your blessings by recording them will cause a blessing explosion in your life. Try it.

Create a Power Playlist.

Create a list of songs from any genre that uplift and empower you. Music is instantly transformational. Music can soothe, uplift, enlighten and encourage you on those days that you feel like giving up. Develop the habit of treating yourself to music therapy for an hour per week.

Reward Yourself. Celebrate Life.

Abundant living requires balance, so carve out time to do things that you enjoy. It doesn't have to cost anything or break your budget. For example, something as simple as a 20-minute walk in the park can work miracles for your spirit and your inner child. Time spent in nature is healing at its best. Don't forget the tried and true bubble bath. There are a thousand ways to pamper yourself, so get creative.

Now hold on with this one. Some of you have been doing nothing but pampering yourself with overspending and overindulging. I am not referring to this type of pampering. However, if this describes your behavior, you will need to seriously examine where that type of behavior is leading you.

Diet and Exercise.

As a personal trainer and life coach, I place great emphasis on diet and exercise. Your body is the physical manifestation of the sum total of your life experience. It is an outward reflection of your inner life. An important part of your healing will involve tweaking your diet. I won't get into details here but at least consider drinking eight glasses of water daily. Eliminate sugary drinks or make Monday a meatless day. These simple changes can bring about clarity and enhance your creativity.

Set Boundaries.

One of the ways that low self-esteem manifests is in people-pleasing and the inability to set boundaries. Often we say 'Yes" when we mean "No." Then we resent having said yes. As Sexual Abuse Survivors we may have to learn how to say "NO." It's okay. Breathe. Practice saying "No" with passion and sincerity. Practice saying "No" with a smile on your face. Say it with me right now. NNNNOOOO. Ahhh. Does it feel scary? Don't worry. The more that you say it, the easier it will become. If you are unsure, buy yourself some time by saying something like:

"I'm not sure that's feasible."

"I'll let you know."

"Let me give that some thought."

Take back your power. Take all the time that you need. Be aware of manipulators, controllers, whiners, guilt-trippers, emotional blackmailers, emotional hitmen/hitwomen and passive aggressors. Learn to feel comfortable with your own decisions. Learn to trust yourself.

For those of you who impose on others or are controlling, reel it in and examine your issues of anger and resentment.

Renewal and the Transformed Mind.

At last the transformation has taken place and friends and loved ones can barely recognize who you are. You are now more peaceful and confident. And you want to stay that way, yes? So continue reading empowering books and listening to empowering audio. There's loads of stuff to listen to on Audible.com or Youtube. Hey! This is the information age. See my recommendations. Continue focusing on things that are lovely and pure. Continue guarding your tongue. Continue monitoring your thoughts because you are now fully aware that you must guard your heart since everything you do flows from it.

MY FORGIVENESS LETTER

Letter to my Inner Child

For the many times that you were afraid, scared, lonely, cringing in the corner, depressed and angry, I apologize.

I am sorry for the many times I did not protect you from unscrupulous people and toxic relationships.

I was wounded and unable to draw clear boundaries. I was wounded and afraid to be alone.

I was wounded and needy - oh so needy. I was wounded and lost so I thought that somebody could fix me. I thought that someone, anyone, could heal the woundedness that I chose to ignore.

I allowed and tolerated inappropriate behavior because I was too weak to stand on my own emotionally.

I deluded myself into thinking that healing was unnecessary.

I pretended that I was all right. I did not trust the fact that with healing I could be made whole again.

Understand that for me it was easier to stay in denial than to face all the work that healing entails.

I apologize for not addressing the emotional damage that was inflicted on you.

I did not know how deeply negative the impact would be on me and those that I love.

I had no idea that those 'bad' things would create codependency, low self-esteem, soul-wrenching pain and actually have a far-reaching multi-generational impact on me and my children.

I understand now that you survived actual soul murder and that I should pay attention when you cry out for attention.

I promise to listen to you when you are sad or crying because I have learned that when I don't, it manifests itself in negative ways in my relationships.

I unconsciously caused myself and others more pain. I now know that you represent the most precious part of me; the part that can be spontaneous and full of joy and creativity but only if I am careful to seek healing.

Forgive me for not taking better care of you.

I did not know any better and when I did realize that you were really hurting, I was too afraid; so I stuffed my feelings. Starting today I promise to send you love.

I promise to listen to you more and address your pain. I promise to protect you. My goal is to be made whole so that you can feel safe.

I know now that without this healing the landscape of my soul will remain a desolate, cavernous wasteland.

I can't wear this mask anymore. I need to be authentic and now is the time. Forgive me - I Love You.

CONCLUSION

Out of the huts of history's shame. I rise.

Up from a past that's rooted in pain. I rise.

Maya Angelou

***

I have written on behalf of a few brave women as well as those forced to remain hidden in the shadows marginalized by religion, rhetoric and dogma like the woman with the 'issue of blood.' (This *is* actually an issue of *blood.* This is an issue of your *blood* relatives betraying you; an issue where your church family "covered by the *blood*" often shaming the victim and protecting the perpetrators.)

This book is by no means an exhaustive guide for healing. For those who will surely criticize this book (and by extension, me) for exposing this 'secret,' I accept your criticism with no resentment. Further to that, I remain unapologetic. Hopefully these words will encourage honest conversations around the impact of incest and childhood sexual abuse on women (and men, for that matter). (Yes. Sadly thousands of men have their stories to tell; stories that I did not feel I could adequately express.)

To my sisters and brothers, whether you choose to share your story or not consider this: It will take all of us working together to bring healing. Always remember that you have greatness within you.

****

Looking back on life I see moments

when the secret of joy became plain to me

and I began to dance its dance.

Alice Walker.

YOU ARE YOUR BEST THING!

FIVE THINGS NEVER TO TELL A SEXUAL ABUSE SURVIVOR

Everything happens for a reason.

Though this may seem well-intentioned, what the SAS actually hears is that in some twisted way they are better off having suffered at the hands of a pedophile. The mental state of the SAS must be addressed in the moment before they are brought to a more empowered state of mind. Evil simply exists in the world. Hurting people hurt people. That's a fact. It may be more beneficial listen non-judgmentally to the story of the broken soul before responding. The Great Physician is the ultimate restorer and healer so don't take responsibility for their healing. It's important for the SAS to know that they are not responsible for having been abused but they are responsible for how they respond. Indeed, a setback can be a setup for incredible growth. Like Maya says, "still like dust, I rise!"

That happened a long time ago.

On the surface, this is factual. The truth is that the soul wound of childhood sexual abuse creates such deep psychic bleeding that left unexamined can last a lifetime. Even the victims of childhood sexual abuse fail to realize the depth of their psychic injuries. Some are stuck at the developmental stage at which their abuse occurred, regardless of their achievements and social appearances. This brokenness is far-reaching. The stain of abuse impacts self-esteem in such a way

that Sexual Abuse Survivors actually choose inappropriate partners to reenact their old stories. Sexual Abuse Survivors may become co-dependent and many are unable to maintain appropriate boundaries in relationships. In that regard, the notion that it "happened a long time ago" is a fallacy. The act occurred long ago but the impact can be ongoing. It's not what happened as much as how we respond to what happened. Avoid making this statement. It is almost always infuriating for a SAS to hear.

I understand how you feel but ...

STOP. Unless you have been sexually abused as a child, you can't possibly understand how it feels. Just don't say it.

Everything is going to be all right.

Hmmm. How do you actually know this? Furthermore, even if everything were going to be 'all right,' the mindset of the sexual abuse survivor at the time of the discussion must be addressed. You have to truly listen and try to understand. By addressing the mindset of the individual at that moment you are acknowledging their true feelings and are better positioned to guide them towards more empowering thoughts. Many Sexual Abuse Survivors are clinically depressed and without treatment things progress to hopelessness and despair. Unless the Sexual Abuse Survivor takes responsibility and does the work, things may in fact worsen.

Just Stop Thinking About It.

Quick. Don't think about a pink elephant in a tutu. See what I mean? It is impossible to just stop thinking about anything. It is possible, however, to encourage the individual to change their focus. Encourage them to focus on whatsoever is good in their lives. Everyone has at least one good thing going on in their lives. Encourage them to discard negative thoughts by reading positive books or repeating positive affirmations or scripture. Development of a renewed mind is a conscious decision. Now that is empowering.

30 EMPOWERING AFFIRMATIONS

You were created in the image of Almighty God. The same God who spoke the universe into being. There is power in the Word of God. And there is power in what you say. One immutable spiritual law declares that, "The tongue has the power of life and death …"

Why does this matter? It matters because despite that fact that you were exploited at a young age, you are responsible for your life now. And this takes courage and discipline. Speak back to negative outcomes with the Word. Dig deep. Tell your spirit man what to expect. Speak to your mountains. This is the only way to evolve into the woman (or man) that God wants you to become. Below are thirty empowering affirmations.

1. I trust the Holy Spirit for guidance and protection.
2. I am Uniquely me and Marvelously made.
3. I am Empowered by the Holy Spirit.
4. I am Loved Deeply by God.
5. have everything that I need for a successful Life.
6. My steps are ordered because I am prayerful.
7. I am released from Toxic Shame.
8. I am fully able to face life's challenges.
9. I take responsibility for my actions today.
10. I am kind and compassionate to everyone that I meet.
11. When I make mistakes, I understand that I am learning and growing. I make mistakes but I am NOT a mistake.
12. I will think before I speak. I respond rather than react.
13. I am a victim no more. I am comfortable in my own power.
14. I never participate in destructive relationships.

15. I live my life powerfully from day to day and no longer delay activities waiting to be rescued.
16. I can identify unhealthy relationships and terminate them accordingly.
17. I allow time to reveal the true nature of every relationship.
18. I practice forgiveness on a daily basis.
19. I am not afraid to ask for help when I need it.
20. I avoid negative people and never participate in gossip.
21. I believe that there is a spiritual solution for every problem.
22. I believe that all things are possible with God.
23. I believe that I deserve the best that life has to offer.
24. I believe that there are more than enough resources available to me so I choose to be charitable always.
25. I forgive my past mistakes and make the most of today.
26. Life can bring pain and disappointment but with God on my side I am more than a Conqueror.
27. I have a right to feel what I feel, even anger. It is my privilege to manage and express how I feel responsibly.
28. I can make it through dark seasons because as I walk through the valley of the Shadow of death, the Holy Spirit comforts, teaches and empowers me.
29. I demonstrate a can-do attitude in all that I do.
30. I am Awesome!

Join us on Facebook

Join the movement of over 8,000 and growing on Facebook.

https://www.facebook.com/listendaddylisten

Please contact me with your thoughts or
comments. I'd love to hear from you.

listendaddylisten@gmail.com.

Printed in the United States
By Bookmasters